50 Appetizers for Korean Families

By: Kelly Johnson

Table of Contents

- Kimchi (Fermented Cabbage)
- Korean Fried Chicken Wings
- Tteokbokki (Spicy Rice Cakes)
- Pajeon (Green Onion Pancakes)
- Japchae (Sweet Potato Noodles)
- Gyeran-jjim (Steamed Egg Custard)
- Mandu (Korean Dumplings)
- Korean BBQ Lettuce Wraps
- Sundubu-jjigae (Soft Tofu Stew)
- Korean Style Pickled Radish (Danmuji)
- Banchan (Side Dishes)
- Korean Style Deviled Eggs
- Sweet and Spicy Garlic Shrimp
- Fish Cake Skewers (Eomuk)
- Mini Kimbap (Rice Rolls)
- Cheesy Corn with Mayonnaise
- Pork Belly Sliders
- Soy Sauce Eggs
- Korean Style Potato Salad
- Gochujang Meatballs
- Spicy Cucumber Salad (Oi Muchim)
- Tempura Vegetables
- Korean Grilled Vegetable Skewers
- Korean Corn Cheese
- Sesame Spinach Salad (Sigeumchi Namul)
- Marinated Beef Skewers (Bulgogi)
- Kimchi Quesadilla
- Sweet Potato Fritters
- Korean Style Meatloaf Bites
- Seaweed Salad
- Stuffed Bell Peppers
- Shrimp and Vegetable Pancakes
- Savory Scallion and Egg Pancakes
- Cheesy Korean Hotdogs
- Korean Style Cabbage Rolls

- Spicy Chicken Wings
- Roasted Chestnuts
- Gochujang Tofu Bites
- Korean Style Salsa
- Korean Spiced Nuts
- Grilled Spicy Sausage Skewers
- Rice Cake Skewers
- Chili Garlic Edamame
- Sweet and Spicy Radish Cubes
- Crispy Seaweed Snacks
- Mini Kimchi Pancakes
- Korean BBQ Meatballs
- Cucumber and Seaweed Rolls
- Sesame Garlic Shrimp
- Vegetable Dumplings

Kimchi (Fermented Cabbage)

Ingredients:

- 1 medium Napa cabbage
- 1/4 cup sea salt
- 4 cups water
- 1 tablespoon grated ginger
- 4 cloves garlic, minced
- 1 tablespoon sugar
- 3 tablespoons Korean red pepper flakes (gochugaru)
- 2 green onions, chopped

Instructions:

1. Cut the cabbage into quarters and remove the core. In a large bowl, dissolve sea salt in water and soak the cabbage for 2 hours, turning occasionally.
2. Rinse the cabbage thoroughly and drain. In a separate bowl, mix ginger, garlic, sugar, and gochugaru.
3. Rub the mixture between the cabbage leaves, then pack into a clean jar, pressing down to release air.
4. Add green onions on top, seal, and ferment at room temperature for 2-5 days. Store in the refrigerator once fermented.

Korean Fried Chicken Wings

Ingredients:

- 2 pounds chicken wings
- 1 cup potato starch
- Oil for frying
- 1/4 cup gochujang (Korean chili paste)
- 1/4 cup honey
- 2 tablespoons soy sauce
- 2 cloves garlic, minced

Instructions:

1. Rinse chicken wings and pat dry. Coat with potato starch.
2. Heat oil in a deep pan to 350°F (175°C). Fry wings in batches for about 10-12 minutes until golden and crispy.
3. In a saucepan, combine gochujang, honey, soy sauce, and garlic over medium heat. Stir until smooth.
4. Toss fried wings in the sauce and serve hot.

Tteokbokki (Spicy Rice Cakes)

Ingredients:

- 1 pound Korean rice cakes (tteok)
- 2 cups water
- 2 tablespoons gochujang
- 1 tablespoon gochugaru
- 1 tablespoon sugar
- 1/2 cup fish cakes (optional)
- 2 green onions, chopped

Instructions:

1. Soak rice cakes in water for 30 minutes if hard.
2. In a pot, combine water, gochujang, gochugaru, and sugar. Bring to a boil.
3. Add the rice cakes and cook for 5-7 minutes until softened.
4. Stir in fish cakes if using and simmer for another 2 minutes.
5. Garnish with green onions before serving.

Pajeon (Green Onion Pancakes)

Ingredients:

- 1 cup all-purpose flour
- 1 cup water
- 1/2 teaspoon salt
- 1 bunch green onions, cut into 2-inch pieces
- Oil for frying

Instructions:

1. In a bowl, mix flour, water, and salt until smooth.
2. Stir in green onions.
3. Heat oil in a skillet over medium heat. Pour in the batter to form a pancake and cook for about 3-4 minutes on each side until golden.
4. Cut into wedges and serve with soy sauce for dipping.

Japchae (Sweet Potato Noodles)

Ingredients:

- 8 ounces sweet potato noodles (dangmyeon)
- 1 tablespoon sesame oil
- 1 carrot, julienned
- 1 bell pepper, sliced
- 1 cup spinach
- 1/2 onion, sliced
- 2 cloves garlic, minced
- 2 tablespoons soy sauce
- 1 tablespoon sugar
- Sesame seeds for garnish

Instructions:

1. Cook sweet potato noodles according to package instructions; drain and set aside.
2. In a large pan, heat sesame oil and sauté garlic and onion until fragrant.
3. Add carrots, bell pepper, and spinach, cooking until tender.
4. Stir in the noodles, soy sauce, and sugar, tossing to combine.
5. Garnish with sesame seeds before serving.

Gyeran-jjim (Steamed Egg Custard)

Ingredients:

- 4 eggs
- 1 cup water
- 1 teaspoon soy sauce
- 1 green onion, chopped
- Salt, to taste

Instructions:

1. In a bowl, whisk together eggs, water, soy sauce, and salt until smooth.
2. Pour the mixture into a heatproof bowl.
3. Steam over simmering water for about 15-20 minutes until set.
4. Garnish with chopped green onion before serving.

Mandu (Korean Dumplings)

Ingredients:

- 1 package mandu wrappers
- 1 cup ground pork or beef
- 1/2 cup tofu, crumbled
- 1/2 cup chopped cabbage
- 2 green onions, chopped
- 2 cloves garlic, minced
- 1 tablespoon soy sauce
- Salt and pepper, to taste

Instructions:

1. In a bowl, combine all filling ingredients.
2. Place a spoonful of filling in the center of each wrapper. Moisten the edges and fold over to seal.
3. Steam or pan-fry dumplings until cooked through, about 8-10 minutes.
4. Serve with soy sauce or dipping sauce.

Korean BBQ Lettuce Wraps

Ingredients:

- 1 pound beef (sirloin or ribeye), thinly sliced
- 2 tablespoons soy sauce
- 1 tablespoon sesame oil
- 2 cloves garlic, minced
- Lettuce leaves (romaine or butter)
- Sliced cucumbers and carrots for garnish

Instructions:

1. Marinate beef in soy sauce, sesame oil, and garlic for at least 30 minutes.
2. Grill or pan-fry the beef until cooked through.
3. Serve the beef in lettuce leaves with cucumbers and carrots for wrapping.

Sundubu-jjigae (Soft Tofu Stew)

Ingredients:

- 1 tablespoon vegetable oil
- 1/2 onion, sliced
- 2 cloves garlic, minced
- 1 green chili pepper, sliced
- 1 cup vegetable broth or water
- 1 package soft tofu (sundubu)
- 1 tablespoon gochujang (Korean chili paste)
- 1 tablespoon soy sauce
- 1 teaspoon sesame oil
- 2 green onions, chopped
- 1 egg (optional)

Instructions:

1. Heat oil in a pot over medium heat. Add onions and garlic, sautéing until fragrant.
2. Stir in the green chili pepper and vegetable broth. Bring to a simmer.
3. Add the soft tofu, breaking it up gently. Stir in gochujang and soy sauce.
4. Simmer for 5-10 minutes, then drizzle with sesame oil and top with green onions.
5. If desired, crack an egg into the stew before serving and let it cook in the hot broth.

Korean Style Pickled Radish (Danmuji)

Ingredients:

- 1 large daikon radish
- 1 cup water
- 1/2 cup rice vinegar
- 1/4 cup sugar
- 1 tablespoon salt
- 1 tablespoon turmeric (for color)

Instructions:

1. Peel the daikon radish and cut it into thin matchsticks or rounds.
2. In a pot, combine water, rice vinegar, sugar, salt, and turmeric. Heat until sugar dissolves.
3. Pour the pickling liquid over the radish in a jar.
4. Let it cool to room temperature, then refrigerate for at least 24 hours before serving.

Banchan (Side Dishes)

Ingredients: (Example selections)

- **Seasoned Spinach:** 2 cups spinach, blanched, and mixed with sesame oil, garlic, and salt.
- **Pickled Cucumbers:** 1 cucumber, sliced, mixed with soy sauce, sugar, and sesame seeds.
- **Radish Salad:** 1 cup diced radish mixed with vinegar, sugar, and chili flakes.

Instructions:

1. Prepare each side dish as directed above.
2. Serve an assortment of banchan in small bowls to accompany a Korean meal.

Korean Style Deviled Eggs

Ingredients:

- 6 hard-boiled eggs
- 3 tablespoons mayonnaise
- 1 teaspoon gochujang
- 1 teaspoon mustard
- 1 teaspoon soy sauce
- 1 green onion, finely chopped
- Sesame seeds for garnish

Instructions:

1. Slice the hard-boiled eggs in half and scoop out the yolks into a bowl.
2. Mash the yolks and mix in mayonnaise, gochujang, mustard, soy sauce, and green onions.
3. Spoon or pipe the mixture back into the egg whites.
4. Garnish with sesame seeds before serving.

Sweet and Spicy Garlic Shrimp

Ingredients:

- 1 pound shrimp, peeled and deveined
- 3 tablespoons gochujang
- 2 tablespoons honey
- 4 cloves garlic, minced
- 1 tablespoon soy sauce
- 1 tablespoon sesame oil
- Green onions for garnish

Instructions:

1. In a bowl, mix gochujang, honey, garlic, soy sauce, and sesame oil.
2. Marinate the shrimp in the mixture for at least 30 minutes.
3. Heat a skillet over medium-high heat and cook the shrimp until pink and cooked through, about 3-4 minutes per side.
4. Garnish with green onions before serving.

Fish Cake Skewers (Eomuk)

Ingredients:

- 1 pound fish cakes, sliced into strips
- 1 tablespoon soy sauce
- 1 tablespoon sesame oil
- 1 tablespoon sugar
- Skewers

Instructions:

1. Preheat a grill or skillet over medium heat.
2. In a bowl, mix soy sauce, sesame oil, and sugar.
3. Thread fish cake strips onto skewers and brush with the sauce.
4. Grill or pan-fry for 3-4 minutes per side until golden.

Mini Kimbap (Rice Rolls)

Ingredients:

- 2 cups cooked rice
- 1 tablespoon sesame oil
- 1 teaspoon salt
- 4 sheets of seaweed (nori)
- Fillings (e.g., cucumber, carrot, pickled radish, egg, and crab sticks)

Instructions:

1. In a bowl, mix rice with sesame oil and salt.
2. Place a sheet of nori on a bamboo mat or flat surface. Spread a thin layer of rice on top, leaving a border.
3. Layer fillings across the rice.
4. Roll tightly and slice into bite-sized pieces.

Cheesy Corn with Mayonnaise

Ingredients:

- 1 can corn (drained)
- 1/4 cup mayonnaise
- 1/2 cup shredded cheese (cheddar or mozzarella)
- 1 tablespoon sugar
- 1 tablespoon chopped green onions

Instructions:

1. In a bowl, mix corn, mayonnaise, cheese, and sugar until well combined.
2. Transfer to a baking dish and bake at 350°F (175°C) for 15-20 minutes until bubbly and golden.
3. Garnish with green onions before serving.

Pork Belly Sliders

Ingredients:

- 1 pound pork belly
- Salt and pepper to taste
- Slider buns
- Sliced cucumbers
- Gochujang mayonnaise (mix gochujang with mayonnaise)

Instructions:

1. Preheat the oven to 300°F (150°C). Season the pork belly with salt and pepper.
2. Place the pork belly in a baking dish and cover it with foil. Bake for 2.5 to 3 hours until tender.
3. Let it cool, then slice into small pieces.
4. Assemble sliders by placing pork belly on slider buns, topping with sliced cucumbers, and adding gochujang mayonnaise.

Soy Sauce Eggs

Ingredients:

- 4 soft-boiled eggs
- 1/4 cup soy sauce
- 1/4 cup water
- 1 tablespoon mirin (optional)
- 1 teaspoon sugar

Instructions:

1. In a bowl, mix soy sauce, water, mirin, and sugar until dissolved.
2. Peel the soft-boiled eggs and submerge them in the marinade.
3. Let them sit for at least 2 hours or overnight for best flavor.
4. Serve as a side dish or snack.

Korean Style Potato Salad

Ingredients:

- 2 cups diced potatoes (boiled and cooled)
- 1/2 cup mayonnaise
- 1 tablespoon mustard
- 1/4 cup chopped carrots
- 1/4 cup chopped pickles
- Salt and pepper to taste

Instructions:

1. In a large bowl, combine boiled potatoes, mayonnaise, mustard, carrots, and pickles.
2. Mix well and season with salt and pepper to taste.
3. Chill in the refrigerator for at least 30 minutes before serving.

Gochujang Meatballs

Ingredients:

- 1 pound ground beef or pork
- 1/4 cup breadcrumbs
- 1 egg
- 2 tablespoons gochujang
- 2 cloves garlic, minced
- Salt and pepper to taste

Instructions:

1. Preheat the oven to 400°F (200°C).
2. In a bowl, mix all ingredients until well combined.
3. Form into small meatballs and place on a baking sheet.
4. Bake for 15-20 minutes or until cooked through. Serve with extra gochujang for dipping.

Spicy Cucumber Salad (Oi Muchim)

Ingredients:

- 2 cups cucumbers, thinly sliced
- 1 tablespoon salt
- 1 tablespoon sugar
- 2 tablespoons gochugaru (Korean red pepper flakes)
- 1 tablespoon soy sauce
- 1 tablespoon sesame oil
- 1 clove garlic, minced
- Sesame seeds for garnish

Instructions:

1. In a bowl, sprinkle cucumbers with salt and let sit for 10 minutes.
2. Rinse and drain the cucumbers.
3. Add sugar, gochugaru, soy sauce, sesame oil, and garlic. Toss to combine.
4. Garnish with sesame seeds before serving.

Tempura Vegetables

Ingredients:

- 1 cup mixed vegetables (carrots, zucchini, bell peppers, etc.)
- 1 cup tempura batter mix
- Ice-cold water
- Oil for frying

Instructions:

1. Heat oil in a deep pan to 350°F (175°C).
2. In a bowl, mix tempura batter with ice-cold water until just combined.
3. Dip vegetables in the batter and fry until golden brown.
4. Drain on paper towels and serve with dipping sauce.

Korean Grilled Vegetable Skewers

Ingredients:

- 2 cups mixed vegetables (bell peppers, zucchini, mushrooms)
- 2 tablespoons soy sauce
- 1 tablespoon sesame oil
- 1 tablespoon gochujang
- Skewers

Instructions:

1. Preheat a grill or grill pan over medium heat.
2. In a bowl, mix soy sauce, sesame oil, and gochujang.
3. Thread vegetables onto skewers and brush with the marinade.
4. Grill for 5-7 minutes until charred and tender.

Korean Corn Cheese

Ingredients:

- 1 can corn (drained)
- 1/2 cup mayonnaise
- 1/2 cup shredded cheese (mozzarella or cheddar)
- 1 tablespoon sugar
- 1 tablespoon chopped green onions

Instructions:

1. Preheat the oven to 350°F (175°C).
2. In a bowl, mix corn, mayonnaise, cheese, and sugar.
3. Pour into a baking dish and bake for 15-20 minutes until bubbly and golden.
4. Garnish with green onions before serving.

Sesame Spinach Salad (Sigeumchi Namul)

Ingredients:

- 1 lb (450 g) spinach
- 2 tsp sesame oil
- 1 tbsp soy sauce
- 1 tbsp toasted sesame seeds
- 1 garlic clove, minced
- 1 tsp salt (for blanching)
- 1 tsp sugar (optional)

Instructions:

1. **Blanch the Spinach:**
   - Bring a large pot of water to a boil. Add 1 tsp salt and the spinach.
   - Blanch the spinach for 30 seconds, then immediately transfer it to an ice water bath to stop the cooking.
2. **Drain and Squeeze:**
   - Drain the spinach thoroughly and gently squeeze out excess water.
   - Place the spinach on a cutting board, chop into 2-3 inch pieces, and transfer to a bowl.
3. **Season the Spinach:**
   - Add sesame oil, soy sauce, minced garlic, sugar (if using), and toasted sesame seeds to the bowl.
4. **Mix and Serve:**
   - Toss the spinach well to coat evenly with the seasoning.
   - Adjust salt to taste if needed.
5. **Garnish and Enjoy:**
   - Sprinkle with a few more sesame seeds before serving. Serve chilled or at room temperature.

This simple and flavorful side dish complements many Korean meals and can be prepared in minutes!

Marinated Beef Skewers (Bulgogi)

Ingredients:

- **1 lb (450 g)** ribeye or sirloin steak, thinly sliced
- **6-8 wooden skewers** (soaked in water for 30 minutes)

Marinade:

- **1/4 cup (60 ml)** soy sauce
- **2 tbsp** brown sugar
- **1 tbsp** honey
- **2 tbsp** sesame oil
- **4 garlic cloves**, minced
- **1/2 pear** or Asian pear, grated
- **1/2 tsp** black pepper
- **1/2 tsp** chili flakes (optional, for heat)
- **1 tbsp** rice vinegar (optional, for added tang)
- **2 green onions**, finely chopped
- **1 tbsp** toasted sesame seeds

Instructions:

1. **Prepare the meat:**
    - Slice the steak against the grain into thin strips (1/4 inch thick). This makes the meat more tender and easy to thread onto skewers.
2. **Make the marinade:**
    - In a bowl, whisk together soy sauce, brown sugar, honey, sesame oil, garlic, grated pear, black pepper, and optional chili flakes. Mix in the chopped green onions and sesame seeds.
3. **Marinate the beef:**
    - Add the beef slices to the marinade, making sure they are well-coated. Cover and refrigerate for **at least 2 hours** (or overnight for the best flavor).
4. **Prepare skewers:**
    - Thread the marinated beef strips onto the soaked skewers. Avoid overcrowding to ensure even cooking.
5. **Cook the skewers:**
    - **Grill method:** Preheat a grill to medium-high heat. Grill the skewers for **2-3 minutes per side**, until the beef is caramelized and slightly charred.

- **Pan-fry method:** Heat a grill pan over medium-high heat and cook the skewers for **2-3 minutes per side**.
6. **Serve:**
    - Garnish with more sesame seeds and chopped green onions. Serve with steamed rice, kimchi, and fresh vegetables for a complete meal.

Kimchi Quesadilla

Ingredients:

- 4 flour tortillas (medium-sized)
- 1 cup kimchi, chopped (drained of excess liquid)
- 1½ cups shredded cheese (mozzarella, cheddar, or a blend)
- 1 tbsp butter or oil (for frying)
- 2 tbsp green onions, chopped (optional)
- 1 tbsp sesame seeds (optional)
- Sriracha or Gochujang (for drizzling)

Instructions:

1. **Prepare the Kimchi** – Chop the kimchi into smaller pieces and drain off excess liquid to prevent the quesadilla from getting soggy.
2. **Heat the Pan** – Heat a skillet over medium heat and add a small amount of butter or oil.
3. **Assemble the Quesadilla** – Place one tortilla in the pan. Sprinkle a layer of shredded cheese on top. Add a generous layer of chopped kimchi. If desired, sprinkle green onions and sesame seeds for extra flavor. Top with another layer of cheese to help bind everything. Place the second tortilla on top.
4. **Cook the Quesadilla** – Cook for 2-3 minutes on each side, pressing lightly with a spatula, until the tortilla is golden brown and the cheese has melted. Repeat the process for the second quesadilla.
5. **Slice and Serve** – Cut the quesadilla into wedges and serve hot with a drizzle of Sriracha or Gochujang for added heat.

Enjoy the fusion of savory, spicy, and cheesy flavors!

Sweet Potato Fritters

Ingredients:

- 2 medium sweet potatoes, peeled and grated
- 1/2 cup all-purpose flour
- 1/4 cup green onions, chopped
- 1 large egg
- 1 tsp garlic powder
- 1/2 tsp salt
- 1/4 tsp black pepper
- Oil for frying

Instructions:

1. In a large bowl, combine the grated sweet potatoes, flour, green onions, egg, garlic powder, salt, and pepper. Mix until well combined.
2. Heat a skillet over medium heat and add oil.
3. Drop spoonfuls of the sweet potato mixture into the hot oil, flattening them slightly with the back of the spoon.
4. Cook for about 3-4 minutes on each side until golden brown. Drain on paper towels before serving.

Korean Style Meatloaf Bites

Ingredients:

- 1 lb ground beef or pork
- 1/2 cup breadcrumbs
- 1/4 cup onion, finely chopped
- 2 tbsp soy sauce
- 1 tbsp sesame oil
- 1 tbsp brown sugar
- 1 clove garlic, minced
- 1/2 tsp black pepper
- 1/4 tsp red pepper flakes (optional)
- 1 egg, beaten

Instructions:

1. Preheat the oven to 375°F (190°C).
2. In a bowl, mix together the ground meat, breadcrumbs, onion, soy sauce, sesame oil, brown sugar, garlic, pepper, red pepper flakes, and beaten egg until well combined.
3. Shape the mixture into small meatloaf bites and place them on a baking sheet lined with parchment paper.
4. Bake for 20-25 minutes or until cooked through and browned on top.

Seaweed Salad

Ingredients:

- 1 cup dried seaweed (wakame or similar)
- 2 tbsp soy sauce
- 1 tbsp rice vinegar
- 1 tsp sesame oil
- 1 tsp sugar
- 1 tbsp sesame seeds, toasted
- 1/4 cup cucumber, thinly sliced
- 1/4 cup carrots, shredded (optional)
- 1 green onion, sliced (optional)

Instructions:

1. Soak the dried seaweed in warm water for about 10 minutes until rehydrated. Drain and squeeze out excess water.
2. In a bowl, mix together the soy sauce, rice vinegar, sesame oil, and sugar until the sugar dissolves.
3. Toss the rehydrated seaweed with the dressing, adding in cucumber, carrots, and green onion if using.
4. Sprinkle with toasted sesame seeds before serving.

Stuffed Bell Peppers

Ingredients:

- 4 bell peppers (any color)
- 1 cup cooked rice
- 1 lb ground beef or turkey
- 1 cup diced tomatoes (canned or fresh)
- 1/2 cup onion, chopped
- 1 tsp garlic powder
- 1 tsp paprika
- 1/2 tsp salt
- 1/4 tsp black pepper
- 1 cup shredded cheese (optional)

Instructions:

1. Preheat the oven to 375°F (190°C).
2. Cut the tops off the bell peppers and remove the seeds.
3. In a skillet, sauté the onion until translucent. Add the ground meat, cooking until browned. Stir in the rice, tomatoes, and seasonings.
4. Fill the bell peppers with the mixture and top with cheese if desired.
5. Place the stuffed peppers in a baking dish and bake for 25-30 minutes until the peppers are tender.

Shrimp and Vegetable Pancakes

Ingredients:

- 1 cup shrimp, peeled and chopped
- 1 cup mixed vegetables (carrots, bell peppers, peas)
- 1/2 cup flour
- 1/2 cup water
- 1 egg
- 1 tsp soy sauce
- Oil for frying

Instructions:

1. In a bowl, mix flour, water, egg, and soy sauce until smooth.
2. Fold in the shrimp and vegetables.
3. Heat oil in a skillet over medium heat.
4. Pour batter into the skillet, forming pancakes. Cook until golden brown on both sides, about 3-4 minutes each.
5. Drain on paper towels before serving.

Savory Scallion and Egg Pancakes

Ingredients:

- 1 cup all-purpose flour
- 1/2 cup water
- 2 eggs, beaten
- 1/4 cup scallions, chopped
- Salt to taste
- Oil for frying

Instructions:

1. In a bowl, combine flour and water to form a batter.
2. Stir in the eggs, scallions, and salt.
3. Heat oil in a skillet over medium heat.
4. Pour batter into the skillet, cooking until set and golden brown on both sides, about 3-4 minutes.
5. Slice and serve warm.

Cheesy Korean Hotdogs

Ingredients:

- 4 hotdogs
- 4 mozzarella cheese sticks
- 1 cup all-purpose flour
- 1/2 cup breadcrumbs
- 1/2 cup cornmeal
- 1 egg, beaten
- Oil for frying

Instructions:

1. Preheat the oil in a deep fryer or large pot.
2. Insert a cheese stick into each hotdog.
3. Dip the hotdogs in flour, then in the beaten egg, and finally coat with breadcrumbs and cornmeal.
4. Fry the hotdogs until golden brown and cheese is melted, about 3-5 minutes.
5. Serve with ketchup or mustard.

Korean Style Cabbage Rolls

Ingredients:

- 1 head of cabbage
- 1 lb ground beef or pork
- 1 cup cooked rice
- 1/2 cup onion, finely chopped
- 2 tbsp soy sauce
- 1 tsp garlic, minced
- Salt and pepper to taste

Instructions:

1. Boil the cabbage leaves in salted water until pliable, about 5 minutes.
2. In a bowl, combine meat, rice, onion, soy sauce, garlic, salt, and pepper.
3. Place a spoonful of the filling in each cabbage leaf and roll tightly.
4. Arrange the rolls in a baking dish, cover with water or broth, and bake at 350°F (175°C) for 30-40 minutes.

Spicy Chicken Wings

Ingredients:

- 2 lbs chicken wings
- 1/4 cup soy sauce
- 2 tbsp gochujang
- 2 tbsp honey
- 1 tbsp sesame oil
- 1 tsp garlic powder

Instructions:

1. In a bowl, mix soy sauce, gochujang, honey, sesame oil, and garlic powder.
2. Add the chicken wings and marinate for at least 30 minutes.
3. Preheat the oven to 400°F (200°C) and place the wings on a baking sheet.
4. Bake for 40-45 minutes, flipping halfway, until crispy and cooked through.

Roasted Chestnuts

Ingredients:

- 1 lb fresh chestnuts

Instructions:

1. Preheat the oven to 425°F (220°C).
2. Cut an "X" in the flat side of each chestnut to prevent bursting.
3. Spread chestnuts on a baking sheet and roast for 20-30 minutes until shells are crispy and chestnuts are tender.
4. Let cool slightly, peel, and serve warm.

Gochujang Tofu Bites

Ingredients:

- 1 block firm tofu, pressed and cubed
- 2 tbsp gochujang
- 1 tbsp soy sauce
- 1 tbsp sesame oil
- 1 tbsp honey or maple syrup
- Oil for frying

Instructions:

1. In a bowl, mix gochujang, soy sauce, sesame oil, and honey.
2. Toss the cubed tofu in the marinade and let sit for 15 minutes.
3. Heat oil in a skillet over medium-high heat.
4. Fry the marinated tofu until golden brown on all sides, about 10 minutes.
5. Serve warm, garnished with green onions if desired.

Korean Style Salsa

Ingredients:

- 2 ripe tomatoes, diced
- 1/2 onion, finely chopped
- 1/4 cup cilantro, chopped
- 1 jalapeño, minced (optional)
- 2 tbsp soy sauce
- 1 tbsp sesame oil
- 1 tbsp rice vinegar
- Salt to taste

Instructions:

1. In a bowl, combine tomatoes, onion, cilantro, and jalapeño.
2. In a separate small bowl, whisk together soy sauce, sesame oil, rice vinegar, and salt.
3. Pour the dressing over the vegetable mixture and stir until combined.
4. Let sit for 15 minutes before serving to allow flavors to meld.

Korean Spiced Nuts

Ingredients:

- 2 cups mixed nuts (almonds, cashews, peanuts)
- 1 tbsp gochugaru (Korean red pepper flakes)
- 1 tbsp soy sauce
- 1 tbsp honey
- 1 tsp sesame oil
- 1/2 tsp garlic powder
- 1/2 tsp salt

Instructions:

1. Preheat the oven to 350°F (175°C).
2. In a mixing bowl, combine all ingredients and stir until the nuts are well coated.
3. Spread the nuts on a baking sheet in a single layer.
4. Bake for 15-20 minutes, stirring occasionally, until golden and fragrant.
5. Allow to cool before serving.

Grilled Spicy Sausage Skewers

Ingredients:

- 1 lb spicy sausage (like chorizo or Korean sausage), cut into chunks
- 1 bell pepper, cut into squares
- 1 onion, cut into squares
- 2 tbsp gochujang
- 1 tbsp soy sauce
- 1 tbsp honey

Instructions:

1. Preheat the grill to medium-high heat.
2. In a bowl, mix gochujang, soy sauce, and honey.
3. Thread sausage, bell pepper, and onion onto skewers.
4. Brush the skewers with the marinade.
5. Grill for 10-12 minutes, turning occasionally, until cooked through.

Rice Cake Skewers

Ingredients:

- 1 lb rice cakes (tteok), sliced
- 1/4 cup gochujang
- 1 tbsp soy sauce
- 1 tbsp honey
- 1 tbsp sesame seeds
- Skewers

Instructions:

1. In a small bowl, mix gochujang, soy sauce, and honey to make a marinade.
2. Thread the rice cake slices onto skewers.
3. Brush the rice cakes with the marinade.
4. Grill or pan-fry the skewers for 5-7 minutes until slightly charred.
5. Sprinkle with sesame seeds before serving.

Chili Garlic Edamame

Ingredients:

- 1 lb edamame (in pods)
- 2 tbsp soy sauce
- 1 tbsp sesame oil
- 2 cloves garlic, minced
- 1 tsp chili flakes
- Salt to taste

Instructions:

1. Boil the edamame in salted water for 5 minutes, then drain.
2. In a bowl, combine soy sauce, sesame oil, garlic, chili flakes, and salt.
3. Toss the drained edamame in the sauce until evenly coated.
4. Serve warm or at room temperature.

Sweet and Spicy Radish Cubes

Ingredients:

- 1 cup daikon radish, peeled and cubed
- 2 tbsp gochugaru
- 1 tbsp sugar
- 1 tbsp soy sauce
- 1 tbsp rice vinegar

Instructions:

1. In a bowl, combine gochugaru, sugar, soy sauce, and rice vinegar to create a dressing.
2. Add the cubed radish to the bowl and toss until well coated.
3. Let sit for at least 30 minutes to allow flavors to develop before serving.

Crispy Seaweed Snacks

Ingredients:

- 1 sheet of nori (seaweed)
- 1 tbsp sesame oil
- 1/2 tsp sea salt

Instructions:

1. Preheat the oven to 300°F (150°C).
2. Brush the nori sheet with sesame oil and sprinkle with sea salt.
3. Cut the nori into squares or strips.
4. Bake for 10-15 minutes until crispy.
5. Allow to cool before serving.

Mini Kimchi Pancakes

Ingredients:

- 1 cup kimchi, chopped
- 1/2 cup all-purpose flour
- 1/4 cup water
- 1 egg, beaten
- 2 green onions, chopped
- 1 tsp sesame oil
- Oil for frying

Instructions:

1. In a bowl, mix kimchi, flour, water, egg, green onions, and sesame oil until combined.
2. Heat oil in a skillet over medium heat.
3. Pour small amounts of batter into the skillet, forming mini pancakes.
4. Cook for 2-3 minutes on each side until golden brown.
5. Drain on paper towels and serve with dipping sauce.

Korean BBQ Meatballs

Ingredients:

- 1 lb ground beef or pork
- 1/4 cup breadcrumbs
- 1/4 cup green onions, chopped
- 2 tbsp soy sauce
- 1 tbsp gochujang
- 1 tbsp sesame oil
- 1 tsp garlic, minced
- 1 egg

Instructions:

1. Preheat the oven to 400°F (200°C).
2. In a bowl, combine all ingredients and mix until well combined.
3. Form the mixture into small meatballs and place on a baking sheet.
4. Bake for 15-20 minutes until cooked through.
5. Serve with a dipping sauce.

Cucumber and Seaweed Rolls

Ingredients:

- 1 cucumber, julienned
- 4 sheets of nori (seaweed)
- 1 cup sushi rice, cooked and seasoned
- Soy sauce for dipping

Instructions:

1. Lay a sheet of nori on a bamboo mat or flat surface.
2. Spread a thin layer of sushi rice over the nori, leaving a small border.
3. Place a line of cucumber strips along the bottom edge of the rice.
4. Roll tightly from the bottom to the top, sealing the edge with water.
5. Slice into pieces and serve with soy sauce.

Sesame Garlic Shrimp

Ingredients:

- 1 lb shrimp, peeled and deveined
- 2 tbsp sesame oil
- 3 cloves garlic, minced
- 1 tbsp soy sauce
- 1 tbsp honey
- 1 tbsp sesame seeds
- 2 green onions, sliced

Instructions:

1. Heat sesame oil in a skillet over medium heat.
2. Add garlic and sauté until fragrant.
3. Add shrimp and cook until pink, about 3-4 minutes.
4. Stir in soy sauce and honey, cooking for an additional minute.
5. Sprinkle with sesame seeds and green onions before serving.

Vegetable Dumplings

Ingredients:

- 1 cup cabbage, finely chopped
- 1 cup mushrooms, chopped
- 1/2 cup carrots, grated
- 2 green onions, chopped
- 1 tbsp soy sauce
- 1 tsp sesame oil
- Dumpling wrappers
- Oil for frying

Instructions:

1. In a bowl, mix cabbage, mushrooms, carrots, green onions, soy sauce, and sesame oil.
2. Place a spoonful of filling in the center of each dumpling wrapper.
3. Moisten the edges with water, fold, and seal.
4. Heat oil in a skillet over medium heat and add dumplings.
5. Fry until golden brown, then add water to the pan, cover, and steam for 5-7 minutes.

www.ingramcontent.com/pod-product-compliance
Lightning Source LLC
LaVergne TN
LVHW081323060526
838201LV00055B/2422